BBC Gardeners' World

POCKET PLANTS

PLANTS FOR SHADE

Andi Clevely

Photographs by
Eric Crichton and Jo Whitworth

BBC Books

Author Biography

Andi Clevely has been a working gardener for nearly thirty years. He began his career in Leeds City Council central nurseries and since then has worked in many gardens around the country, including Windsor Great Park. He is now responsible for a country estate and large garden in Stratford-on-Avon where he lives with his wife. Andi has written a number of gardening books and is a regular columnist for *Homes & Gardens* magazine.

Acknowledgements

The publishers would like to thank Colgrave Seeds, West Adderbury, Banbury Oxfordshire for their assistance with the photography. Photographs on pages 51 and 68 © Brian Carter (Garden Picture Library). Photographs on pages 6, 10, 12, 14, 20, 22, 23, 26, 27, 28, 32, 36, 37, 39, 40, 41, 42, 45, 46, 47, 48, 54, 57, 59, 60, 63, 65, 69 and 76 © Eric Crichton. Photograph on page 50 © Ron Evans (Garden Picture Library). Photograph on page 29 © Steven Wooster (Garden Picture Library). Photographs on pages 8, 11, 13, 15, 16, 18, 19, 21, 25, 30, 33, 34, 49, 52, 56, 67, 70, 71 and 74 © BBC (Eric Crichton). Photographs on pages 7, 9, 17, 24, 31, 35, 38, 43, 44, 53, 55, 58, 61, 62, 64, 66, 72, 73, 75, 77, 78, 79 and 80 © BBC (Jo Whitworth).

Published by BBC Books,
an imprint of BBC Worldwide Publishing.
BBC Worldwide Limited, Woodlands,
80 Wood Lane, London W12 0TT.

First published 1997
© BBC Worldwide Limited 1997
The moral right of the author has been asserted

ISBN 0 563 38778 5

Photographs by Eric Crichton and Jo Whitworth

Artworks by Pond and Giles

Set in Futura

Printed and bound in Belgium by Proost NV
Colour separations by Radstock Reproductions Limited, Midsomer Norton, Avon
Cover printed in Belgium by Proost NV

Common Names

INTRODUCTION

Shade can actually be a great asset in a garden, allowing us to grow plants with longer flowering seasons, with softer colours and greater charm, subtle leaf textures or delicate leaves that would be scorched in bright sunlight. Making the most of a shady spot is simply a matter of selecting those plants that prefer subdued light, cooler growing conditions and shelter from severe weather. As this book shows, there is a wealth of attractive species to choose from so you should have no problem selecting the right plants for your garden.

Degrees of shade

Semi-shade The majority of shaded sites have partial, dappled or light shade, where sunlight may penetrate for less than half the day, or is filtered and softened by thin tree foliage. Most of the plants included in this book enjoy this type of position. You can even create these conditions where necessary, by planting a small tree or shrub to cast the light shade desired.

Full shade A little more challenging are those areas where sunlight is almost completely excluded, perhaps by a nearby building or an evergreen tree overhead. There are fewer suitable plants, but you can often expand the choice by thinning branches, painting a dark wall white, or cunningly installing a mirror or a light-coloured paving or mulch. Some variegated plants succeed here and help relieve the darkness.

Types of shade plants

Shrubs and Climbers: Some are deciduous and others evergreen, but all are valuable for providing permanence and volume in shaded positions.

Foliage plants: Most tend to be woodland plants, thriving in the wild on dry or moist shade, and some are natural mat-forming plants which make good ground-cover. They provide contrast and interest, all year if they are evergreen. Variegated kinds show up well in shade, while a plain dark variety makes a good background for flowering plants.

Herbaceous flowers: Perennial flowers that naturally grow in woodland shade are often early-flowering, or start into growth early in the year to take advantage of the light before tree are fully out. Some like sunlight for part of the day, and enjoy the dappled shade beneath taller plants, whereas others prefer deeper shade all the time. Note that some need acid or alkaline soils.

Bulbs: There are many bulbs and bulbous plants adapted to growing beneath trees, and these are all suitable for shady gardens. Many flower and die down early and can be combined with ground-cover foliage plants or herbaceous flowers for extended colour.

Preparing the ground

Soil conditions vary enormously in shaded sites, and sometimes planting sites need special preparation.

Dry shade: Soils here can be thin and lifeless, especially close to high walls, or beneath trees and hedges.Thoroughly dig the area and work in as much organic material as possible – garden compost, leafmould or well-rotted manure are all suitable. Annual mulches of the same materials will help the new plants to survive.

Moist shade: This often needs less attention. Simply forking over the ground and adding garden compost will be enough for most woodland, bog and marginal plants that enjoy cool damp conditions. For a plant that likes a moist but well-drained position, you might need to improve the drainage by adding grit, or some similar coarse material.

Planting

Container-grown specimens can be planted at any season if the soil is not too wet or frozen. Bare-rooted shrubs, foliage plants and herbaceous flowers are normally planted while dormant, between early autumn and early spring; evergreens are planted in mid-autumn or mid-spring. Plant spring bulbs in autumn, and autumn-flowering kinds in mid- to late summer.

With most species you can follow the same simple procedure, but check details in the individual entries.

- A few weeks beforehand, prepare the ground thoroughly according to the type of shade.

- Dig a hole large enough to accommodate the roots without cramping them, and at the same depth as the plant was previously growing. Bury bulbs at a depth 2-3 times the height of the dry bulb.

- Replace the well-crumbled soil and firm gently into place.

Care

Watering: Unless the ground is already very moist, water thoroughly immediately after planting and continue watering regularly until plants are growing strongly. Thereafter dry shade species will normally cope on their own, but water occasionally in an exceptionally dry season. Moist shade plants need consistently damp soil and should be soaked every 2-3 weeks in dry weather.

Feeding: Most species benefit from annual feeding, either a mulch of garden compost or well-rotted manure in autumn or spring, or a topdressing of general fertilizer in spring as growth revives.

Mulching: Apart from feeding plants, a mulch prevents rapid evaporation and helps soils retain moisture. Grass clippings from untreated lawns, autumn leaves and shredded bark are all suitable mulching materials for spreading around plants in autumn or in late spring once the soil has warmed up.

ACONITUM NAPELLUS

An old cottage garden flower, cultivated since the sixteenth century for its herbal value (but note that plants are very poisonous). Excellent in wild-flower gardens, and also tolerates sunny sites, although growth is then less impressive.

Flowering time: Late summer and early autumn.

Foliage: Glossy, dark green, divided and palm-shaped.

Height: 1.2–1.8m (4–6ft)

Spread: 30cm (12in)

Positioning: 30cm (12in) apart, in semi-shade on moist soils in flower borders; also shaded meadows and orchard turf.

Planting time: Autumn or spring.

Propagation: Sow seeds in spring in a cold frame; divide roots autumn or spring.

Care: Mulch in late spring with lawn clippings or garden compost. May need staking and protection from slugs and rabbits. Feed once or twice during growth to encourage good stems, and divide every 4–5 years to maintain vigour.

Recommended: Basic species; also soft pink 'Carneum' and white form 'Albidum'. Also *A. variegatum*, (pale blue or blue-white), and *A. vulparia* (syn. *A. lycoctonum* spp. *vulparia*) with pale yellow flowers and elegant foliage.

Ajuga reptans Bugle, Carpenter's Herb

Flowering time: Late spring and early summer.

Foliage: Small, oval and shiny, arranged in neat rosettes.

Height: 15cm (6in)

Spread: 30cm (12in)

Positioning: 15cm (6in) apart, as ground cover for moist shade, on banks or edges of borders. It associates well with dwarf bulbs and grasses, and thrives in fertile soil under hedges.

Planting time: Autumn or spring.

Propagation: Sow seeds in spring or autumn, barely covered in trays in a cold frame; divide rosettes in autumn or spring.

Care: Undemanding, but water in dry weather. Spreads by 30cm (12in) runners and may need division every 3–4 years.

Recommended: 'Atropurpurea' (rich purple) for light shade only; 'Variegata' (green, white and grey leaves), best in full shade.

AJUGA REPTANS

A wild creeping plant of woodland glades. It provides neat and colourful non-invasive ground cover, especially for herb gardens where it was once grown medicinally for treating cuts and other wounds.

ALCHEMILLA MOLLIS

A beautiful plant of woodland margins, popular for flower arranging and informal plantings, and the ideal foil for yellow, blue or purple flowers. After rain both the leaves and flower heads retain drops, which glisten in the sunlight.

Flowering time:	Early and mid-summer.
Foliage:	Pleated, downy and rounded, greyish-green and elegant.
Height:	30–45cm (12–18in)
Spread:	60cm (24in)
Positioning:	30cm (12in) apart, in mixed borders and as ground cover, especially under shrubs; makes a fine edging to shaded paths.
Planting time:	Autumn or spring.
Propagation:	Sow seeds in spring in a cold frame; divide plants autumn or spring; also self-sown seedlings.
Care:	Mulch in spring with garden compost, and support growth with twiggy sticks if plants tend to flop. Deadhead before seeds are ripe to prevent self-seeding.
Recommended:	Basic species, and 'Grandiflora' with larger flowers; also *A. alpina*, smaller with bluish foliage, and *A conjuncta*, darker green.

Anemone nemorosa Wood Anemone

ANEMONE NEMOROSA

Flowering time:	Early and mid-spring.
Foliage:	Bright medium-green and intricately cut (dies down by mid-summer).
Height:	15cm (6in)
Spread:	30cm (12in)
Positioning:	8cm (3in) deep and 20cm (8in) apart, in large groups in light or heavy soil enriched with plenty of compost or leaf mould; on banks and under trees or shrubs.
Planting time:	Autumn or spring.
Propagation:	Ripe seeds sown in late summer in situ or in a cold frame; divide plants in spring.
Care:	Undemanding. Cover with a little leaf litter in autumn.
Recommended:	Normal species; also 'Alba Plena' (double white), 'Bowles' Purple' and 'Robinsoniana' (pale blue). *A. × hybrida*, the Japanese Anemone, also thrives in shaded flower borders. Best forms include 'Honorine Jobert' (white) and 'Queen Charlotte' (purple, semi-double).

The first of the spring anemones to flower, and charming in naturalized drifts, especially when associated with primroses, bluebells, columbines or cranesbills. Quickly colonizes sites when it is happy.

Aquilegia vulgaris Columbine, Granny's Bonnet

AQUILEGIA VULGARIS

Unlike the vividly coloured hybrids of sunlit borders, the common columbine is a native of woodland shade and a popular wild flower since Saxon times. The dumpy short-spurred flowers are usually blue, but pink and white forms often appear from self-set seeds.

Flowering time: Late spring to mid-summer.

Foliage: Elegantly divided and blue-green, tinged pink when young.

Height: 60–90cm (2–3ft)

Spread: 45cm (18in)

Positioning: 30cm (12in) apart, in fairly fertile soil with a little lime; in groups in borders, beside hedges, and in dappled shade under trees or shrubs.

Planting time: Spring.

Propagation: Sow seeds in situ in spring or early autumn.

Care: Adequate moisture is important, so add plenty of humus when preparing the soil, and soak plants occasionally in a dry season. Deadhead if free seeding is likely to be a nuisance. Mulch in early spring with compost or leaf mould.

Recommended: Normal species; also many garden forms including A. v. 'Nivea' (Munstead White Columbine) with grey foliage, pretty 'Hensol Harebell', and double 'Nora Barlow'; brighter colours prefer full sun.

Flowering time: Mid- and late spring.

Foliage: Glossy green and arrow-shaped ('Marmoratum' marbled with grey and cream), appearing from late autumn onwards.

Height: 45cm (18in)

Spread: 30cm (12in)

Positioning: 10cm (4in) deep and 23cm (9in) apart, in most soils, where they get sun in winter and shade in summer; ideally beside hedges and under deciduous trees. Try combining them with hellebores and snowdrops.

Planting time: Late summer.

Propagation: Divide tubers in late summer; also take small offsets from main tuber, for growing on.

Care: Mulch with leaf mould just as new leaves appear in late autumn.

Recommended: This is the best form for decorative value; for shaded wild gardens A. maculatum (Lords and Ladies) is a suitable alternative, stunning in autumn when its berries are ripe.

ARUM ITALICUM 'PICTUM'

The ornamental leaves of this form are the prime attraction – they start into growth just when there is little else in the garden and remain fresh all winter. The spikes of bright scarlet berries (very poisonous) are a further highlight. (syn. A. i. ssp. italicum.)

ARUNDINARIA VIRIDISTRIATA

Just one of many bamboos that revel in partial shade, and possibly the best of the variegated kinds. It is not as invasive as some species, forming attractive small patches of slim canes no more than 5mm (¼in) in diameter. (syn. *Pleioblastus auricomus, P. viridistriatus.*)

Flowering time:	Rarely occurs.
Foliage:	Dark green and hairy, variably striped with rich yellow (often more yellow than green), up to 20cm (8in) long, on erect purple-green canes.
Height:	1.8m (6ft), less in semi-shade
Spread:	90cm (3ft)
Positioning:	30–45cm (12–18in) apart, sheltered from cold winds; as ornamental groups and screens.
Planting time:	Late winter or spring.
Propagation:	Divide in late spring; take 15cm (6in) cuttings of runners, and insert vertically, in late winter or early spring.
Care:	Cut old canes to ground level in autumn to encourage fresh young foliage.
Recommended:	Selected forms 'Bracken Hill' and *A. v. chrysophyllus*; also *Pleioblastus pygmaeus*, dwarf species, spreads readily as ground cover.

Astilbe × arendsii Hybrid Astilbe

ASTILBE × ARENDSII 'AMETHYST'

Flowering time: Mid- to late summer.

Foliage: Dainty and fern-like, bronze-green when unfurling, and later light or dark green according to flower colour.

Height: 60cm–1.2m (2–4ft)

Spread: 60–90cm (2–3ft)

Positioning: 45–60cm (18–24in) apart, in moist soils (not clay or chalk), well fortified with garden compost; in groups in beds and borders, especially associated with irises.

Planting time: Autumn or spring.

Propagation: Sow seed mixtures under glass in spring; divide plants (essential for named varieties) in mid-autumn or spring.

Care: Mulch with well-rotted manure or garden compost in autumn, and water lavishly in dry weather. Flowering declines with age, so divide and replant every 3–4 years.

Recommended: Numerous good forms such as 'Amethyst'; 'Bergkristall' (white); 'Cattleya' (pink); 'Feuer' (syn. 'Fire'), red; 'Weisse Gloria' (white).

Given plenty of organic humus and moisture, these lovely and hardy plants will thrive happily, making large ornamental bushes. The flower spikes last for many weeks, and look handsome even after fading.

13

ASTRANTIA MAJOR

Long-lived perennials with the subtle charm of wild flowers, and popular with flower arrangers as the cut blooms last well and may be dried for winter use. Best grown in the moist dappled shade of woodland margins.

Flowering time: Early to late summer.
Foliage: Dark green and shiny, interestingly cut and palmate.
Height: 60cm (24in)
Spread: 45cm (18in)
Positioning: 30cm (12in) apart in semi-shade and fertile soils with a little lime, in moist borders and beside water.
Planting time: Autumn or spring.
Propagation: Sow seeds in a cold frame in mid-spring; divide roots in late autumn or early spring.
Care: Undemanding. Water in dry weather and mulch with compost in spring on lighter soils. Mark positions of plants in winter as they vanish from sight.
Recommended: Basic form and coloured selections such as *A. m. alba*, 'Claret', *A. m. rosea* and *A. m. rubra*; also daintier *A. minor* and *A. carniolica* var. *rubra* (red); variegated forms are best in full sun. *A. maxima* can be up to 90cm (3ft) high with shell-pink flowers The hybrid 'Hadspen Blood' has dark pinkish-red flowers.

ATHYRIUM FILIX-FEMINA

Flowering time: Foliage plant only.

Foliage: Light green, elegant and lacy.

Height: 90cm (3ft)

Spread: 75–90cm (2½–3ft)

Positioning: 60cm (2ft) apart, in moist but well-drained soil with plenty of humus; in shaded borders, walls and beside paths.

Planting time: Spring.

Propagation: Surface-sow spores under glass in autumn; divide plants in spring.

Care: Water occasionally in dry weather. Do not clear the withered fronds until spring as they protect the dormant crowns over winter. May attract slugs.

Recommended: Basic species, and any decorative form such as 'Corymbiferum', 'Frizelliae' and 'Plumosum'; also *A. nipponicum* var. *pictum*, (Painted Lady Fern) with silvery mottled fronds. *A. pycnocarpon* (Glade Fern) is another shade-lover, up to 75cm (30in) high, with very attractive fronds.

Cool and impressive, especially in summer when the delicately cut foliage is a refreshing foil for coloured flowers such as fuchsias. There are many forms with tasselled, divided or plumed fronds, all desirable and tolerant of pollution.

Aucuba japonica Laurel

AUCUBA JAPONICA 'CROTONIFOLIA'

Tough, handsome and resistant to pollution from traffic, Aucubas are mostly seen in their striking variegated forms. Usually male and female flowers are on separate bushes and both are needed (or grow a bisexual variety) for berries.

Flowering time: Mid-spring.

Foliage: Large, pale or mid-green, bright and shiny.

Height: 2.4–3.6m (8–12ft)

Spread: 3m (10ft)

Positioning: Light or medium shade (any variegation may pale in deeper shade); as a specimen bush, hedge or windbreak.

Planting time: Autumn or mid-spring.

Propagation: Take semi-ripe cuttings from young shoots in mid-summer; take hardwood cuttings in autumn.

Care: Undemanding. May be left unpruned, or trimmed hard in mid-spring with secateurs (cut leaves turn brown). Clip hedges mid-summer.

Recommended: Plain form; also many variegated varieties, such as 'Crotonifolia', narrow leaves, small spots; 'Picturata', dark leaves, large blotches; 'Rozannie', bisexual with good berries; 'Variegata' (syn. 'Maculata'), large spots and blotches.

Bergenia 'Elephant's Ears'

Flowering time: Early to late spring, sometimes again early autumn.

Foliage: Large, leathery and rich green, some turning yellow, scarlet and mahogany in autumn and winter.

Height: 30–45cm (12–18in)

Spread: 45–60cm (18–24in)

Positioning: 30cm (12in) apart, in virtually any position, including exposed windy sites; in beds and borders, and as ground cover.

Planting time: Autumn or spring.

Propagation: Divide after flowering or in autumn.

Care: Little needed. Remove dead leaves in early spring, and mulch with compost on lighter soils before flowers appear. Divide after 4–5 years.

Recommended: Plain species such as *B. cordifolia* or *B. crassifolia*, and their cultivated forms, including 'Ballawley' (red), 'Bressingham White', 'Morgenröte' (syn. 'Morning Red'), 'Purpurea', 'Silberlicht' (syn. 'Silver Light').

BERGENIA 'EVENING BELLS'

A good survivor, tolerating spartan conditions and so a useful foliage plant where hostas and other less robust plants fail. Some leaves colour in autumn and are good for arrangements, as are the dense heads of long-lasting blooms. (syn. *Bergenia* 'Abendglocken'.)

Brunnera macrophylla

BRUNNERA MACROPHYLLA

A common and easily pleased garden perennial with loose racemes of long-lasting flowers similar to those of forget-me-nots. After flowering the attractive foliage develops into lavish mounds, which are effective as ground cover.

Flowering time: Mid-spring to early summer.

Foliage: Large, dark green and heart-shaped.

Height: 38–45cm (15–18in)

Spread: 60cm (24in)

Positioning: 45cm (18in) apart, in most kinds of fertile soil; in borders or woodland shade, and as ground cover under shrubs, where the foliage will persist well into autumn. Variegated forms are less robust and succeed best away from competition, in shaded containers for example. All forms make excellent edging for large borders.

Planting time: Autumn.

Propagation: Sow seeds in a cold frame in spring; divide plants in autumn; take root cuttings in winter.

Care: Mulch in spring. Blackened leaves protect crowns in winter, so do not clear until spring.

Recommended: Basic species; also 'Betty Bowring' (syn. *B. m. alba*); 'Hadspen Cream' and 'Langtrees'.

Camellia × williamsii Camellia

Flowering time: Late winter to mid-spring.

Foliage: Dark and glossy, pointed with serrated edges.

Height: 1.8–3m (6–10ft)

Spread: 1.8–3m (6–10ft)

Positioning: Light shade in warmer regions, full sun in cold climates, but not where they receive the morning sun; best in lime-free, leafy soil. May be grown against walls or in tubs.

Planting time: Spring.

Propagation: Layer in early spring.

Care: Mulch in spring with garden compost or leaf mould. Water when dry with rainwater, especially from late summer when buds are forming. Deadhead regularly, and prune only to remove dead wood and restore shape, in winter or spring.

Recommended: Many good forms, including 'Anticipation' (crimson), 'Debbie' (rose-pink), 'J C Williams' (single pink), 'Leonard Messel' (apricot pink).

CAMELLIA × WILLIAMSII 'DONATION'

A large variety, and perhaps the best twentieth-century hybrid, with vigorous erect growth. It is slow-growing, but after several decades can reach the dimensions of a small or medium-sized tree. The warmer the climate, the more shade it finds acceptable.

19

CAMPANULA GLOMERATA

A lovely and colourful wild flower of chalklands, happy in full sun or light shade and producing a spectacular display grown *en masse* in almost any soil, but especially those of low fertility.

Flowering time:	Mid- to late summer.
Foliage:	Rough, stalkless, broad and lance-shaped.
Height:	30–45cm (12–18in)
Spread:	15cm (6in)
Positioning:	15cm (6in) apart, in any well-drained soil with a little lime; in borders and wild gardens, and also as ground cover beneath roses, in wild-flower meadows and rockeries.
Planting time:	Autumn or spring.
Propagation:	Sow seeds on the surface in a cold frame in autumn; divide plants in spring.
Care:	Deadhead to encourage repeat flowering and to prevent seeding, which can be lavish.
Recommended:	Basic species; also *C. g.* var. *alba*, 'Purple Pixie', 'Schneekrone' (syn. 'Crown of Snow'), and large-flowered 'Superba'. Others ideal for well-drained shade include *C. lactiflora*, 1.2m (4ft) tall, with sprays of pale blue flowers, and *C. persicifolia* (Willow Bell) with white or blue flowers.

Chaenomeles speciosa
Flowering Quince, Japanese Quince

Flowering time: Early to mid-spring.

Foliage: Small, shiny and oval, usually appearing after the first flowers, on branching thorny stems.

Height: 3m (10ft)

Spread: 2.4m (8ft)

Positioning: In almost any soil, in an open border or trained against a wall; try combining with a summer-flowering clematis for later colour; may be grown 60cm (2ft) apart for hedging.

Planting time: Spring or autumn.

Propagation: Sow seeds in autumn in a cold frame (variable, mainly red plants); take soft cuttings in early summer under glass; layer in the autumn.

Care: Mulch in autumn with garden compost. Prune back to flower buds in early spring, wall train plants again in summer to leave 2–3 buds of new growth.

Recommended: Many good forms including 'Apple Blossom', 'Geisha Girl' (pink/yellow), 'Nivalis' (white), 'Simonsii' (deep red).

CHAENOMELES SPECIOSA CV

One of the earliest spring-flowering shrubs, and also one of the easiest, performing well in full sun but more eye-catching in light shade. Can be trained flat against a wall, as a dense hedge and also as a free-standing shrub.

CHOISYA TERNATA

A favourite for its spicy, sweetly scented blooms, although the foliage is also strongly aromatic when crushed. Being natives of Mexico the shrubs are often injured by cold winds, and need a warm sheltered site to reach a great size.

Flowering time: Mid- to late spring, and occasionally again in autumn.

Foliage: Dark green, glossy and aromatic.

Height: 1.5–2.7m (5–9ft)

Spread: 1.5–2.1m (5–7ft)

Positioning: In most soils, with light shade and shelter from cold winds; in warm beds and borders, against a warm wall or in containers.

Planting time: Spring or early summer.

Propagation: Take soft cuttings in early summer and grow under glass; take hardwood cuttings in autumn in a cold frame.

Care: Mulch in late spring. Cut back some of the branches after flowering to encourage new basal growth. Move container plants into shelter in autumn.

Recommended: Basic species; also 'Aztec Pearl', slim leaves and larger flowers, and 'Sundance' with golden foliage easily scorched by sunlight and cold winds.

Cimicifuga racemosa Bugbane

Flowering time: Mid-summer to mid-autumn.

Foliage: Fresh green, elegant and divided, in stately clumps.

Height: 1.8m (6ft)

Spread: 60cm (2ft)

Positioning: 45cm (18in) apart, in moist leafy soil; in shaded beds and borders and also in the wild garden.

Planting time: Autumn or spring.

Propagation: Sow seeds in a cold frame in early autumn; divide plants in early spring.

Care: Mulch in early summer with grass clippings or leaf mould, and water in dry seasons.

Recommended: Basic species, and form 'Purpurea'; also *C. dahurica* (autumn-flowering), *C. rubifolia* (taller, cream flowers), and *C. simplex* 'Atropurpurea' (red-brown young foliage). *C. ramosa* is an impressive species, up to 2.1m (7ft) tall and flowering in autumn, its spikes of white flowers towering above the large divided leaves.

CIMICIFUGA RACEMOSA

As the common name suggests, once used to drive away insects, but better known as an early-flowering perennial for the back of the border or for wilder parts of the garden. Combines well with hardy fuchsias and ferns.

Convallaria majalis Lily-of-the-Valley, May Lily

CONVALLARIA MAJALIS

A natural woodlander that might sulk if offered unsuitable sites, but once happy the long thong-like roots will spread energetically, carpeting the ground with fragrant nodding stems of pretty bells.

Flowering time: Mid- to late spring.
Foliage: Large, glossy green and lanceolate, 2–3 arising from the base of each stem.
Height: 20–23cm (8–9in)
Spread: 30cm (12in) or more
Positioning: 20cm (8in) apart and 5cm (2in) deep, in groups in deep moist leafy soil; in lightly shaded borders as ground cover under shrubs or deciduous trees; combines well with columbines and peonies.
Planting time: Autumn.
Propagation: Sow ripe berries (poisonous) in a cold frame in late summer; divide rhizomes in mid-autumn.
Care: Undemanding once established. Mulch in autumn with compost or leaf mould, and divide every 3–4 years.
Recommended: Basic species or *C. m.* var. *rosea* (pale pink); also 'Albostriata' (white-striped leaves), 'Fortin's Giant' (large flowers), *C. m.* var. *variegata* (gold-banded leaves).

Cornus canadensis Creeping Dogwood

Flowering time: Late spring and early summer.

Foliage: Neat, oval and semi-evergreen, often turning red or purple in autumn.

Height: 15–20cm (6–8in)

Spread: 90cm (3ft)

Positioning: Sandy open soil with some humus; in light shade as ground cover in shrub borders and under deciduous trees.

Planting time: Autumn or spring.

Propagation: Divide creeping rootstock in autumn or spring.

Care: Undemanding. Mulch lightly with leaf mould in autumn. May become invasive where conditions are ideal, and should then be divided every 4–5 years.

Recommended: Species only. Taller *Cornus* species for dappled shade include variegated forms of *C. alba*, such as 'Elegantissima' and 'Spaethii', both best on chalky soils. On more acid soils try *C. florida* (Eastern Flowering Dogwood), especially 'Apple Blossom' and 'White Cloud'.

CORNUS CANADENSIS

An unusual dogwood that cannot decide whether it is a semi-evergreen dwarf shrub or a herbaceous perennial. The leafy shoots form attractive carpets starred with conspicuous white flowers that are followed by heads of scarlet berries.

Cotoneaster horizontalis Deciduous Cotoneaster

COTONEASTER HORIZONTALIS

Low and spreading, with arching stems arranged in a characteristic herring-bone pattern, attractive when trained flat against a shaded wall. The small red flowers are popular with bees, while the bright orange-red fruits attract birds in autumn and winter.

Flowering time: Early summer.
Foliage: Small, oval and shiny rich green, in neat pairs along stems.
Height: 60–90cm (2–3ft), up to 3m (10ft) on a wall
Spread: 1.8m (6ft) or more
Positioning: Most well-drained soils; as ground cover in semi-shade or trained against a wall; also clipped as a low hedge.
Planting time: Autumn.
Propagation: Sow ripe berries outdoors in autumn; grow semi-ripe cuttings in a cold frame in summer; grow hardwood cuttings in a cold frame in autumn or winter.
Care: Undemanding. Remove dead wood and unwanted branches in winter; may also be cut hard back to shape in winter.
Recommended: Basic species; also 'Variegatus' (syn. *C. atropurpureus* 'Variegatus'), green and cream leaves but fewer berries and less vigorous.

Crocus tommasinianus Crocus

CROCUS TOMMASINIANUS

Flowering time:	Late winter.
Foliage:	Long and wispy, needle-like with a pale green stripe.
Height:	10cm (4in)
Spread:	10cm (4in)
Positioning:	10cm (4in) apart and 8cm (3in) deep, in natural groups; in light shade beneath shrubs or best in shady turf under deciduous trees
Planting time:	Autumn.
Propagation:	Divide clumps in autumn; also self-seeds freely.
Care:	Little care needed. Leave foliage to die down, and do not mow naturalized colonies until the leaves have completely withered. Divide overcrowded clumps every few years.
Recommended:	Basic species and white form 'Albus'; also garden forms 'Lilac Beauty', 'Ruby Giant' and 'Whitewell Purple'. Most others need full sun, although early flowering *C. chrysanthus* and *C. laevigatus* often succeed at the edge of light shade under trees and shrubs.

Affectionately known as "Tommies", these are some of the earliest crocuses to bloom, in colours varying from pale lavender to purple, with vivid orange stamens like the saffron crocus. Always plant generously and allow to multiply.

Cyclamen hederifolium Wild Cyclamen

CYCLAMEN HEDERIFOLIUM

The leaves alone would recommend these tiny plants for naturalized ground cover in dappled shade, while the first prettily reflexed flowers announce the end of summer. Despite the plants' graceful habit and tiny size, their tubers may reach the size of a small plate. (syn. *C. neapolitanum*.)

Flowering time: Late summer to mid-autumn.

Foliage: Variable in shape, mostly dark green with silvery-grey marbling, from early autumn until late spring.

Height: 10–15cm (4–6in)

Spread: 10cm (4in)

Positioning: 15cm (6in) apart and 2.5–5cm (1–2in) deep; in drifts at the foot of deciduous trees or large shrubs

Planting time: Mid-summer to early autumn.

Propagation: Divide clumps in mid-summer; sow fresh seeds in late spring, in a cold frame or scattered in situ.

Care: Best left undisturbed, when plants will self-seed freely. In mid-summer sprinkle with fine leaf mould or garden compost and a little bonemeal.

Recommended: Basic species and white 'Album'. For ground cover in late winter and early spring grow *C. coum* with grey-green or silvery mottled leaves, and flowers that vary from ivory white to rich magenta.

Flowering time: Late spring and early summer.

Foliage: Bluish-green, finely cut and ferny, on fragile, almost succulent stems.

Height: 60cm (24in)

Spread: 45cm (18in)

Positioning: 30cm (12in) apart, in a cool moist spot with shade during the hottest part of the day, sheltered from winds and late frosts; associates well with ferns.

Planting time: Autumn or spring.

Propagation: Sow seeds in early spring under glass; divide plants in autumn or early spring.

Care: May be slightly temperamental. Best left undisturbed where it is happy, since the roots are very fragile. Mulch with garden compost in autumn, and protect against slugs.

Recommended: Basic species and white form 'Alba'; also D. formosa, with brighter foliage and pink flowers, and D. eximia, a smaller plant for shaded rock gardens.

DICENTRA SPECTABILIS

A delicate and romantic old plant of cottage gardens that needs careful positioning to satisfy its needs. When happy it is a charming sight, but plants die down after flowering and need suitable companions to fill the space afterwards.

Digitalis purpurea (Common) Foxglove

DIGITALIS PURPUREA

An amiable wild flower that will seed itself cheerfully once introduced, with white, pale pink and rich red forms all appearing in surprising places. Seedlings are easily moved while young, though, and can be gathered into informal groups.

Flowering time: Early and mid-summer.
Foliage: Pale green, oval, pointed and softly hairy, arranged in a rosette.
Height: Up to 1.8m (6ft)
Spread: 30–45cm (12–18in)
Positioning: 30cm (12in) apart in bold groups, best in moist semi-shade (but tolerates dry conditions) with shelter from strong winds; in large borders and herb gardens, woodland settings and wild gardens.
Planting time: Autumn.
Propagation: Sow seeds in spring in a cold frame, to flower the following year; plants self-seed freely.
Care: Usually biennial but if prevented from seeding may survive for several years. Add plenty of humus to the soil before planting, and again as a mulch the following spring.
Recommended: Basic species and white 'Alba'; also selected garden forms such as 'Excelsior Hybrids' and 'Gloxiniaeflora', with large open blooms.

Flowering time: Mid-spring to early summer.

Foliage: Large, heart-shaped, glossy and toothed, changing colour from bronze-pink to deep green and then to red as the season progresses.

Height: 30cm (12in)

Spread: 45cm (18in)

Positioning: 30cm (12in) apart, in any reasonable soil in cool semi-shade; as early-flowering ground cover, especially in the shade of trees.

Planting time: Autumn or spring.

Propagation: Divide plants in autumn or spring. May be divided and replanted every few years to accelerate spread.

Care: Water well during the first season. Work a light mulch of garden compost between the stems each spring.

Recommended: Species only; also *E. pubigerum*, taller with leathery leaves, and red-flowered *E. x rubrum*.

EPIMEDIUM PERRALDERIANUM

This is as effective as ivy for dense ground cover under trees, making brilliant fresh green carpets for much of the year. Growth is slow at first, but established clumps soon fill out as the shallow rhizomes start to spread.

Flowering time: Mid-winter to early spring.

Foliage: Wide and deeply divided, some leaves form collars under the flowers.

Height: 5–8cm (2–3in)

Spread: 8cm (3in)

Positioning: 5cm (2in) deep, in groups of 6–8 spaced 15–20cm (6–8in) apart, in light or semi-shade around shrubs and tree trunks.

Planting time: 'In the green' in late spring, or as dry tubers in early autumn.

Propagation: Divide plants after flowering; plants self-seed freely, or fresh seeds may be scattered broadcast.

Care: Plants tolerate dry shade but benefit from occasional watering in a dry spring. Top-dress with compost or leaf mould after leaves die down, and divide congested clumps occasionally (replant immediately).

Recommended: Basic species; also 'Flore Pleno' (double) and bright 'Guinea Gold'.

ERANTHIS HYEMALIS

In the dead of winter these golden flowers, appearing before their leaves, brighten up the gloomy days and last for several weeks before giving way to other spring bulbs. Plant generously, especially dry tubers (many of which may not grow).

Euonymus fortunei Evergreen Euonymus

EUONYMUS FORTUNEI 'EMERALD 'N' GOLD'

Flowering time: Insignificant; grown as a foliage plant.

Foliage: Shiny and oval, with gold edges that become cream flushed with pink in winter.

Height: 90cm (3ft), up to 3m (10ft) on a wall

Spread: Up to 3m (10ft)

Positioning: In most fertile soils, in semi-shade or full shade (but gold colour may fade); as specimens, ground cover, trained on walls or planted 30–38cm (12–15in) apart as a hedge.

Planting time: Autumn or spring.

Propagation: Grow semi-ripe cuttings under glass in summer; grow hardwood cuttings in a cold frame in winter.

Care: Undemanding. Cut back first year's growth by one-third to encourage bushy growth; thereafter prune to shape in spring.

Recommended: Other good varieties include 'Blondy' (pale yellow spots), 'Emerald Gaiety' (greyish with white edges), 'Silver Queen' (white edges), 'Sunspot' (bright yellow).

A quick-growing and low-maintenance shrub for covering the ground or a shady wall on which the new branching shoots develop self-clinging roots. All varieties are ideal for adding coloured highlights among other shrubs.

33

Euphorbia amygdaloides Wood Spurge, Rattlesnake Weed

EUPHORBIA AMYGDALOIDES

A perfect evergreen for poor soils in dry shade, but equally at home in richer, moister conditions. A robust and spreading plant that makes durable ground cover, with 2.5cm (1in) green flowers in spring. (syn. *E. robbiae*.)

Flowering time: Late spring.

Foliage: Tough, rounded and dark green, in rosettes on purplish stems.

Height: 60cm (2ft)

Spread: 60cm (2ft)

Positioning: 45cm (18in) apart, in light soils; as groups in a large border or as ground cover.

Planting time: Spring or early autumn.

Propagation: Divide plants after flowering. Stems exude a milky sap which can be a skin irritant.

Care: Mulch with compost in late winter. Divide every 3–4 years.

Recommended: Although this species is sometimes sold as *E. robbiae*, botanists distinguish a form *E. amygdaloides* var. *robbiae*, which is ideal for carpeting poor ground in dry shade. Other forms of *E. amygdaloides* include 'Rubra' and 'Variegata' although neither form is as robust as the simple species; also good for shade are red-flowered *E. griffithii*, especially 'Dixter' and 'Fireglow', and tall *E. sikkimensis*.

Fatsia japonica Japanese Aralia

Flowering time: Autumn.

Foliage: Large, glossy green and palm-shaped, on long stalks.

Height: 3–4m (10–13ft)

Spread: 2.4m (8ft)

Positioning: In moist well-drained soils in light or full shade; as specimen plants in sheltered corners or against a warm wall, especially in towns and coastal gardens.

Planting time: Early summer after fully hardening off.

Propagation: Take tip cuttings and grow in heat in summer.

Care: Water in dry weather and feed every spring with a general fertilizer. Until established, protect from hard frost by mulching the roots and covering top growth with fleece or bubble plastic.

Recommended: Plain green species; also any variegated form in very mild areas only.

FATSIA JAPONICA

Although often sold and grown as a large house plant, this soon grows into a large handsome foliage shrub if sheltered from cold winds and frosts. The autumn flowers are spectacular creamy heads that last for several weeks.

FUCHSIA

Most fuchsias are slightly tender and used outdoors only for seasonal bedding, but they are superb plants for light shade if protected from cold winds. The so-called hardy fuchsias may be cut down by frost but survive to sprout again in spring.

Flowering time:	Early to late summer.
Foliage:	Pale to mid-green, oval and pointed with a clear central vein.
Height:	Up to 1.5m (5ft)
Spread:	90cm (3ft)
Positioning:	Fertile and well-drained, moist and partially shaded with shelter from cold winds; as specimen bushes in mixed borders, summer bedding and containers, and in mild gardens as hedges.
Planting time:	(Hardy) spring; (tender) early summer.
Propagation:	Grow softwood cuttings under glass any time during the season.
Care:	Take in tender varieties before the first frosts. Protect the roots of outdoor plants with a thick mulch of bracken, straw or leaves over winter; cut off dead stems in mid-spring and prune hedges in late spring.
Recommended:	Hardy: *F. magellanica* and its forms such as 'Alba', 'Gracilis', 'Variegata', 'Pumila' and 'Riccartonii'.

Galanthus nivalis Snowdrop

Flowering time: Late winter to early spring.
Foliage: Slim and grassy, bluish-green.
Height: 15–23cm (6–9in)
Spread: 15cm (6in)
Positioning: 20cm (4in) apart and 20cm (4in) deep, in groups in moist soil, tucked in corners which the flowers will illuminate; also under shrubs, trees and hedges.
Planting time: 'In the green' in late spring, or as dry bulbs in early autumn.
Propagation: Divide immediately after flowering; sow ripe seeds broadcast in situ.
Care: Best in moist fertile soils, so mulch with compost or leaf mould in autumn and feed in spring with bonemeal. Sometimes vigorous clumps become congested after 3–4 years and these may be divided after flowering.
Recommended: Basic species and double form 'Flore Pleno'; also G. elwesii (good on dry soils) and G. 'S. Arnott' (strongly scented).

GALANTHUS NIVALIS

There are many expensive kinds available, but even the plain single snowdrop produces the most welcome display early in the year, and if left undisturbed will spread into robust clumps that bear enough blooms for picking.

Galium odoratum Sweet Woodruff, Kiss-Me-Quick

GALIUM ODORATUM

A semi-evergreen herb that can creep darkly over large areas in moist or dry shaded corners, and then erupt in early summer with stems of bright starry flowers. Cut these for drying to enjoy the scent of new-mown hay. (syn. *Asperula odorata*.)

Flowering time:	Early summer.
Foliage:	Dark green and shiny, in neat whorls like ruffs.
Height:	30–38cm (12–15in)
Spread:	30cm (12in)
Positioning:	15cm (6in) apart, in groups as ground cover in herb gardens, beside paths and under shrubs and trees. Best where the dense mats can spread freely, so avoid planting near or between choicer species that may be over-run after a few seasons.
Planting time:	Any time.
Propagation:	Sow seeds in late summer in situ or in a cold frame; divide plants any time, although best in spring.
Care:	Mulch in spring with garden compost. Cut down top growth in autumn or winter if weather-beaten. Plants are shallow rooting and easily controlled if they become invasive: chop around clumps with a spade and fork out surplus runners. Cut flowering stems in early summer and dry in shade for herbal use.
Recommended:	Basic species only.

Garrya elliptica Garrya

Flowering time: Mid- and late winter.
Foliage: Dark green, oval and leathery, with incised veins.
Height: 3–3.9m (10–13ft)
Spread: 3m (10ft)
Positioning: Most well-drained soils, with a little protection from winter winds, in sheltered shrubberies and against walls. Tolerates polluted and salt-laden air, so ideal for town and seaside gardens.
Planting time: Autumn or spring.
Propagation: Grow hardwood cuttings in late summer or early autumn in a cold frame; layer in autumn.
Care: Mulch in spring with garden compost. Prune in spring, cutting up to one-third of the older stems to prevent overcrowding. May look dull when not in flower, so use to support a mid-season clematis such as 'Bees Jubilee' that is pruned at the same time.
Recommended: Basic species, and 'James Root' (longer tassels, over 30cm (12in) long).

GARRYA ELLIPTICA

A tough shrub, coping with most sites although slightly tender in very exposed positions. Male plants bear the familiar long tassels and are striking in winter, while the females have long chains of dark fruits in summer.

Gentiana asclepiadea Willow Gentian

GENTIANA ASCLEPIADEA

A reliable and long-lived gentian, one of the easiest to grow especially in moist shaded soils where it attains its full size and beauty, growing vigorously into good-sized clumps. Normally pure blue, with occasional white stripes, but attractive in any form.

Flowering time: Mid-summer to early autumn.

Foliage: Long, rich green willow-like leaves along arching stems, with flowers in their axils.

Height: 60–90cm (2–3ft)

Spread: 60cm (2ft)

Positioning: Cool moist soil is essential, with light or semi-shade; in borders and woodland areas, and beside water.

Planting time: Spring.

Propagation: Sow ripe seeds in pots and leave outdoors all winter; divide plants in spring. Plants normally set ample seed, and this should be gathered and sown as soon as ripe. Save and trial all seedlings as worthwhile variations in colour or flowering regularly occur.

Care: Undemanding, and if left alone improves from year to year. Mulch in spring on drier sites.

Recommended: Basic species; also forms such as 'Alba' (white), 'Knightshayes' (white-throated), dwarf and 'Rosea' (rose-pink).

Geranium phaeum Dusky Cranesbill, Mourning Widow

Flowering time: Mid-spring to early summer.

Foliage: Medium green, deeply cut and divided, almost palm-shaped.

Height: 45–60cm (18–24in)

Spread: 30cm (12in)

Positioning: 30cm (12in) apart, in light free-draining soils in semi-shade (or full sun); in informal groups in borders or as ground cover under shrubs and trees.

Planting time: Spring.

Propagation: Sow seeds in a cold frame in late summer or spring; divide plants in spring.

Care: Undemanding. Mulch with compost in autumn, and divide overcrowded clumps every few years.

Recommended: Basic species; also many garden forms, including white 'Album', red *G. p.* var. *lividum* and 'Langthorn's Blue'. Other species suitable for cool shade include *G. endressii* (bright pink) and its garden forms, and also violet-blue *G. pratense* Meadow Cranesbill.

GERANIUM PHAEUM

A remarkable herbaceous geranium that will naturalize itself where content. The pleasing foliage is unusually evergreen, while the small flowers are a dramatic deep crimson, almost black, and look very impressive in solid masses.

Hedera hibernica Irish Ivy

HEDERA HIBERNICA

Ivies are good ground cover plants that can tolerate long periods of drought and thrive where grass fails. This is one of the best and most vigorous, with a distinct flowering stage, quite different in appearance from the earlier growth. (syn. *H. helix* 'Hibernica'.)

Flowering time: Greenish and insignificant umbels in autumn, followed by black berries.

Foliage: Large, dark green and lustrous, five-lobed in early stages and unlobed or heart-shaped on flowering shoots.

Height: Up to 7.5m (25ft)

Spread: 3m (10ft) or more

Positioning: Any soil, in dry full or semi-shade; as ground cover and on structurally sound walls.

Planting time: Autumn or spring.

Propagation: Grow tip cuttings in summer in a cold frame; layer in autumn.

Care: Little needed, except to trim back over-enthusiastic growth whenever necessary.

Recommended: Basic species, and many good garden forms such as 'Deltoidea' (neat, rounded foliage) or variegated 'Anne Marie' and 'Maculata'; also *H. helix* (English Ivy) and its numerous forms.

Helleborus orientalis Lenten Rose

Flowering time: Late winter to mid-spring.
Foliage: Fan-shaped with coarse serrated leaf segments, on stout stems.
Height: 45–60cm (18–24in)
Spread: 60cm (24in)
Positioning: 45cm (18in) apart, in fertile alkaline soil in semi-shade or full sun; on the edge of shrubberies or in shady corners, and also in containers.
Planting time: Autumn or spring.
Propagation: Sow seeds in autumn or spring in a cold frame; divide plants in autumn or spring.
Care: Undemanding. Mulch with garden compost or leaf mould after flowering, and feed with bonemeal. Move container plants under cover in winter to protect roots from freezing.
Recommended: Very variable, with many named forms and groups of hybrids, all of them lovely and worth growing. H. niger (Christmas Rose) also thrives in shade.

HELLEBORUS ORIENTALIS

Long-lived perennials that flower early in the year in a wide range of beautiful colours. The blooms are large, often 8cm (3in) across, and very hardy. Plants self-seed freely, often producing unusual forms that are always worth growing on.

43

Hosta fortunei

HOSTA FORTUNEI

A collective name for a group of decorative Asiatic hybrids, all of them highly attractive foliage plants with the bonus of tall spires of blooms like hyacinths. Particularly successful next to water and in tall terracotta pots.

Flowering time: Mid- to late summer.

Foliage: Long and pointed, grey-green or variegated, deeply veined and slightly translucent.

Height: 45–60cm (18–24in)

Spread: 60cm (24in)

Positioning: 60cm (24in) apart, in cool moist soils with plenty of humus; in shaded borders and shrubberies, beside water and in containers.

Planting time: Spring.

Propagation: Divide in early spring before leaves appear.

Care: Mulch with garden compost or leaf mould in spring before leaves appear, and keep moist in dry seasons. Guard against slugs and snails.

Recommended: Basic species (grey-green leaves), plus 'Albomarginata' (large white-edged leaves), and var. *Albopicta* (golden-yellow with green edges), var. *Aureomarginata* (green with yellow margins), and var. *Hyacinthina* (green leaves, dense flowers).

Hydrangea macrophylla Lacecap Hydrangea

Flowering time: Mid-summer to early autumn.

Foliage: Large, oval and pointed, rich green with pale veins.

Height: Up to 3m (10ft)

Spread: 3–4m (10–14ft)

Positioning: Light shade in moist positions sheltered from hard frosts; in shrubberies, mixed borders, against walls and in large containers.

Planting time: Autumn or spring.

Propagation: Grow semi-ripe cuttings under glass in summer.

Care: Mulch with compost in spring and water in dry weather. Deadhead in spring and prune lightly to shape, cutting out all dead, weak and crowded stems. If leaves turn yellow, treat with sequestered iron.

Recommended: Many garden forms, including: Hortensia – 'Altona' (rose), 'Ami Pasquier' (deep red), 'Madame Emile Mouillère' (white), 'Parzival' (crimson); Lacecap – 'Geoffrey Chadbund' (brick red), 'Lanarth White', 'Tricolor' (pale pink).

HYDRANGEA MACROPHYLLA 'BLUE WAVE'

Lacecap and Hortensia (mophead) hybrids are all forms of *H. macrophylla*, and in most cases flourish in dappled shade. In slightly alkaline soils flower colours may be changed by using a proprietary blueing agent containing aluminium.

HYPERICUM CALYCINUM

The ideal ground cover for challenging sites in dry shade, where the tough plants can spread into dense mats with all-year-round interest and a long season of brilliant golden yellow blooms up to 8cm (3in) across.

Flowering time: Early summer to early autumn.

Foliage: Rich green, large, oval and neat.

Height: 45–60cm (18–24in)

Spread: 90cm–1.8m (3–6ft)

Positioning: 45cm (18in) apart, on dry difficult soils, especially as ground cover under trees or large shrubs. As growth can be invasive, do not plant near choice subjects that may be overwhelmed.

Planting time: Autumn or spring.

Propagation: Divide plants in spring.

Care: Cut down old foliage in spring to encourage plenty of flowers, and then feed with a general fertilizer. Clumps may become invasive and need chopping to size with a spade. Treat outbreaks of rust with systemic fungicide.

Recommended: Basic species only; try also *H.* 'Hidcote' (taller, with large flowers) and *H.* x *moserianum* 'Tricolor' (variegated, for moist shade only) and *H. androsaemum* (Tutsan).

Iris foetidissima Gladdon, Stinking Iris

Flowering time: Early summer.

Foliage: Long, narrow and dark green, strongly pungent if bruised, with several short stalked leaves.

Height: 60cm (24in)

Spread: 45cm (18in)

Positioning: 30cm (12in) apart, in any soil, in light or semi-shade with protection from severe frosts; especially good under trees.

Planting time: Late summer.

Propagation: Sow seeds in situ in autumn; divide plants any time, but best done immediately after flowering.

Care: Undemanding. Plant the rhizomes at, or level with, the soil surface. Flowers and seedheads are good for cutting.

Recommended: Basic species, 'Citrina' (larger flowers) and 'Variegata' (cream-striped leaves), and white-seeded 'Fructu Albo'. I. germanica and its many forms will tolerate dry shade under trees, and I. pseudacorus (Yellow Flag) accepts moist semi-shade.

IRIS FOETIDISSIMA

A well-known wild iris, widely naturalized throughout Europe. Despite its common name, which refers to the smell produced if plants are damaged, it is a desirable curiosity, the subdued flowers giving way to bright orange seeds that last for months.

Jasminum nudiflorum · Winter(-flowering) Jasmine

JASMINUM NUDIFLORUM

The hardiest of the jasmines and the best for growing on a shaded wall or as trailing ground cover. Although deciduous, the stems are evergreen adding winter colour and an effective complement to the bright flowers that are excellent for cutting.

Flowering time: Mid-autumn to late winter.

Foliage: Dark green, oval and shiny, appearing after the flowers.

Height: Up to 3m (10ft)

Spread: 3m (10ft)

Positioning: Any reasonable soil, in light shade; trained against a wall or cascading down a bank, or free-standing (with support) as a weeping shrub.

Planting time: Autumn or spring.

Propagation: Grow semi-ripe cuttings in mid-summer under glass; grow hardwood cuttings with a heel in a cold frame in late autumn; layer in autumn.

Care: Peg down shoots if used to carpet banks, and train climbers on wires. Prune immediately after flowering, removing one-third of the oldest stems and shortening younger shoots as required.

Recommended: Basic species, and 'Aureum' (yellow-blotched leaves).

Leucojum aestivum Summer Snowflake, Loddon Lily

Flowering time: Mid- to late spring.
Foliage: Bright green, long and strap-like.
Height: 50–60cm (20–24in)
Spread: 23cm (9in)
Positioning: 15cm (6in) apart and 10–20cm (4–8in) deep (deepest on light soils), in damp or wet sites; in groups in borders or bog gardens. Also tolerates drier sites if well shaded from the brightest sunlight.
Planting time: Early or mid-autumn.
Propagation: Divide after foliage has died down; dig up bulblets at dividing time and grow on in trays in a cold frame.
Care: Needs little attention. Water in very dry seasons. Initial soil preparation is important as plants prefer a deep root-run. Dig or fork sites a spit deep and add plenty of leaf mould or garden compost before planting.
Recommended: Basic species or larger-flowered 'Gravetye Giant'. L. vernum (Spring Snowflake) and late L. autumnale also enjoy moist shade.

LEUCOJUM AESTIVUM

Slightly misnamed, as it finishes flowering just as summer starts. The green-tipped white bellflowers are carried in nodding groups, up to ten at a time at the ends of the arching stems. In moist soils plants multiply freely into large clumps.

Lilium Lily

LILIUM

Many lilies like their roots in cool shade and their flowers in the sun, but a number of species are happy and multiply in woodland shade, where they look effective planted in natural groups and drifts that suit their handsome informality.

Flowering time: Early summer to early autumn.

Foliage: Mid-green, narrow and pointed, arranged around the flowering stems.

Height: 90cm–1.8m (3–6ft)

Spread: 15–23cm (6–9in)

Positioning: Informal groups in very well-drained soil with a high humus content; in light shade in mixed borders and shrubberies, in containers and under deciduous trees.

Planting time: Late summer or early autumn.

Propagation: Sow seeds in a cold frame in autumn; grow scales from bulbs in boxes or a nursery bed at planting time.

Care: Leave plants to self-seed, but cut down all top growth when quite dead. Mulch in spring with garden compost or leaf mould.

Recommended: *L. hansonii* (orange), *L. henryi* (apricot), *L. martagon* (purple) and white form 'Album', *L. superbum* (orange), *L. lancifolium* syn. *L. tigrinum* (orange-red, spotted), *L. pyrenaicum* (yellow).

Lonicera pileata Privet Honeysuckle

Flowering time: Late spring.
Foliage: Glossy dark green, narrowly elliptical, sometimes semi-evergreen.
Height: 60cm (2ft)
Spread: 1.8m (6ft)
Positioning: Any fertile well-drained soil, in semi-shade or full sun; planted 60cm (2ft) apart as ground cover or as a low hedge; also useful for underplanting tall shrubs.
Planting time: Autumn or spring.
Propagation: Grow semi-ripe cuttings under glass in mid-summer; grow hardwood cuttings in a cold frame in late autumn.
Care: Shorten growth by a third after planting, and trim to shape annually in mid-spring.
Recommended: Basic species and bright-leaved 'Moss Green'; deciduous climbing honeysuckles like *L. x tellmanniana* (copper yellow flowers) and *L. tragophylla* (bright yellow) succeed in semi- or full shade.

LONICERA PILEATA

A low dense shrub, horizontally branching to form good ground cover that retains its leaves in most years. Although mainly a foliage plant, it bears tiny creamy-white flowers followed by translucent violet berries in clusters.

51

LYSIMACHIA NUMMULARIA

Sometimes an irrepressible weed of greenhouses, this little creeper is a delightful ground cover plant with its prostrate evergreen stems studded in summer with bright yellow flowers, 2.5cm (1in) across. Excellent underplanting for dwarf conifers.

Flowering time: Early and mid-summer.
Foliage: Small rounded leaves like coins, with prominent veins, bright green on creeping stems.
Height: 5cm (2in)
Spread: 30cm (12in)
Positioning: Any ordinary soil, preferably moist but tolerates drier sites; as ground cover on walls, banks and beside water, and also in hanging baskets and other containers.
Planting time: Autumn or spring.
Propagation: Grow tip cuttings under glass in summer; divide runners in autumn or spring.
Care: Undemanding, but restrain invasive tendencies by pulling off unwanted stems.
Recommended: Basic species (golden form 'Aurea' needs full sun); creeping *L. nemorum* and tall *L. punctata* (Yellow Loosestrife) are also good in semi-shade. *L. ephemerum* is one of the few grey-leaved plants to enjoy shade.

Mahonia aquifolium Purple Oregon Grape

Flowering time: Late winter to mid-spring.

Foliage: Deep green with reddish stalks, several toothed leaflets in pairs, turning rich purple in winter.

Height: 1.2m (4ft)

Spread: 1.5m (5ft)

Positioning: Almost any soil (prefers moist shade but will tolerate dry sunny positions); as ground cover under trees or specimen shrubs.

Planting time: Autumn or spring.

Propagation: Grow semi-ripe cuttings under glass in summer.

Care: Shorten stems immediately after flowering to encourage bushy growth, and remove one-third of old stems in early summer. Cut back ground cover hard every other year. If plants become invasive, chop back to size with a spade

Recommended: *M. aquifolium* has polished green leaves, *M. a.* 'Apollo' has larger flowers; leaves of *M. a.* 'Smaragd' are bronze when young.

MAHONIA AQUIFOLIUM 'ATROPURPUREA'

A particularly attractive form of the oregon grape, hardiest of all the Mahonias. It is a strong spreading plant that eventually becomes almost impenetrable when grown as ground cover. The dense golden flower clusters are followed by blue-black berries.

MECONOPSIS CAMBRICA

Charming and self-sufficient, seeding itself cheerfully wherever it fancies. It is graceful and ornamental, often flowering through-out the season with large 5cm (2in) papery blooms that vary from pale lemon yellow to rich orange.

Flowering time:	Mid-spring and intermittently throughout summer.
Foliage:	Fresh green, soft and lobed in handsome mounds.
Height:	30–45cm (12–18in)
Spread:	30cm (12in)
Positioning:	23cm (9in) apart in groups in almost any soil, moist or dry, in semi-shade or full sun; in borders and rock gardens, and on walls; combines well with ferns.
Planting time:	Early autumn.
Propagation:	Sow ripe seeds in a cold frame; plants seed freely and seedlings may be transplanted while still young.
Care:	Completely undemanding, but deadhead regularly if self-set seedlings are likely to be a nuisance.
Recommended:	Basic species; also double 'Flore Pleno' and red 'Frances Perry'. Temperamental *M. betonicifolia* (Blue Poppy), also thrives in light shade, as will *M. grandis* and their beautiful joint hybrid *M. × sheldonii*.

Narcissus cyclamineus Cyclamen Narcissus

NARCISSUS CYCLAMINEUS

Flowering time: Late winter and early spring.

Foliage: Long, slim, blue-green and strap-like.

Height: 10–20cm (4–8in)

Spread: 15cm (6in)

Positioning: 15cm (6in) apart and 10cm (4in) deep, naturalized in groups, in moist leafy soil (preferably slightly acid); in semi-shaded beds, borders and grass.

Planting time: Early autumn.

Propagation: Sow ripe seeds in a cold frame in summer (plants self-seed freely); divide clumps after leaves die down.

Care: Allow foliage to die down altogether before mowing colonies naturalized in grass. Dress with bonemeal at planting time and every spring afterwards.

Recommended: Basic species only available; there are many good hybrids between this and large trumpet daffodils, including 'Dove Wings', 'February Gold', 'Jack Snipe', 'Jenny' and 'Peeping Tom'.

One of the most beautiful of all the species narcissi, and also one of the earliest to flower, its rich yellow blooms droop with long trumpets and its petals fold right back to give an almost frightened appearance.

Osmanthus × burkwoodii Osmanthus

OSMANTHUS × BURKWOODII

A hardy and valuable evergreen, with a vigorous upright habit especially useful for hedging. Plants grow slowly at first, so buy as large a specimen as possible. The white or cream trumpet-shaped flowers are pleasantly fragrant. (syn. × *Osmarea burkwoodii*.)

Flowering time: Mid- to late spring.
Foliage: Dark green, oval, glossy and leathery.
Height: 3m (10ft)
Spread: 3m (10ft)
Positioning: Semi-shade or sun, with shelter from cold winds, on most fertile, well-drained soils, but especially on dry chalky ground; ideal as specimen shrubs or trained against a wall, and as hedging planted 60cm (2ft) apart.
Planting time: Autumn or spring.
Propagation: Grow semi-ripe cuttings under glass in summer; grow hardwood cuttings in a cold frame in mid-autumn; layer in autumn.
Care: Trim to shape after flowering, removing up to two-thirds of each young shoot, or hard prune in mid-spring (plants tolerate cutting into old wood).
Recommended: Basic species only; *O. delavayi* (dark grey-green leaves) and *O. heterophyllus* (holly leaves, autumn flowers), and its many garden forms, are worth trying in semi-shade.

Pachysandra terminalis Japanese Spurge

PACHYSANDRA TERMINALIS

Flowering time: Mid-spring.

Foliage: Light green and roughly diamond shaped, clustered at the shoot tips in neat shrubby clumps.

Height: 30cm (12in)

Spread: 45cm (18in)

Planting time: Autumn or spring.

Positioning: 30cm (12in) apart, in moist semi-shade (tolerates dry ground) on most soils, but preferably slightly acid; ground cover and for underplanting shrubs.

Propagation: Grow semi-ripe cuttings under glass in summer; divide plants in autumn.

Care: Cut back the foliage in spring to encourage dense growth. However, annual pruning may not be necessary if growth rate is satisfactory. Cut back excessive spread with a spade.

Recommended: Basic species, and garden forms 'Green Carpet' (dwarf) and 'Variegata' (silver-grey leaves, white edges), although these are slightly tender in exposed positions.

A slowly creeping perennial and one of the best for ground cover in many situations. The fleshy, spreading rhizomes gradually build up a solid low mass of fresh appealing foliage that is reliably evergreen. The flowers are insignificant.

Paeonia officinalis Double Red Peony

PAEONIA OFFICINALIS 'RUBRA PLENA'

One of the oldest peonies, cultivated since the Middle Ages for its herbal value and still a favourite for cottage gardens. Plants are very long-lived and may be naturalized informally; the flowers are strongly perfumed.

Flowering time: Late spring and early summer.

Foliage: Rich green and deeply cut into 3 divided leaflets.

Height: 60cm (24in)

Spread: 60cm (24in)

Positioning: Fertile and well-drained soils, slightly alkaline, in light shade or full sun; as specimen plants in borders, herb gardens and wild gardens.

Planting time: Autumn.

Propagation: Carefully divide the fleshy roots in autumn.

Care: The blooms are heavy, so support the foliage with twiggy sticks in mid-spring. Mulch in autumn with garden compost.

Recommended: Also attractive are the double white 'Alba Plena' and double pink 'Rosea Plena', anemone-flowered 'Anemoniflora Rosea' and the attractive dwarf *P. o.* ssp. *microcarpa*; white *P. emodi*, 90cm (3ft), also likes shade.

Parthenocissus henryana — Chinese Virginia Creeper

Flowering time: Summer (small and insignificant), followed by small bright blue berries in autumn.

Foliage: Large and palm-shaped, with 3–5 oval leaflets, dark green with prominent silver veining.

Height: 4.5m (15ft) or more

Spread: 3m (10ft) or more

Positioning: Moist soil, fertile and well-drained, in shade or semi-shade; on walls and scrambling into trees.

Planting time: Autumn or spring.

Propagation: Grow semi-ripe cuttings under glass in late summer; take hardwood cuttings in spring; layer in autumn or spring.

Care: May need early support with wires or wall nails until reliably self-clinging. May be pruned any time during the growing season if the strong growth exceeds its bounds

Recommended: Basic species only; *P. quinquefolia* (Virginia Creeper) and *P. tricuspidata* (Boston Ivy), especially *P. t.* 'Lowii' and 'Veitchii'.

PARTHENOCISSUS HENRYANA

A perennial vine of exceptional beauty, especially in autumn, and best in shade as sunlight will fade the subtle leaf patterns. One of several vigorous kinds, all self-supporting by means of tendrils that end in sticky pads.

Phlox paniculata Phlox

PHLOX PANICULATA

The true *Phlox paniculata* is a more robust and healthy plant than the common highly bred varieties that must have full sun. The softer-coloured forms are ideal for informal gardens, and fill the air in late summer with their fragrance.

Flowering time: Late summer.
Foliage: Rich green, narrow and pointed, arranged in pairs on wiry stems.
Height: 1.2m (4ft)
Spread: 60cm (2ft)
Positioning: 45–60cm (18–24in) apart, in rich moist soil that remains cool in summer; in lightly shaded borders and wild gardens.
Planting time: Autumn or spring.
Propagation: To avoid eelworm, grow root cuttings under glass in late winter; also divide healthy plants in spring.
Care: Mulch with garden compost or well-rotted manure in spring, and water in very dry seasons. Cut out weaker shoots on large clumps, and shorten outer stems in early summer to improve display.
Recommended: Basic mauve or lilac species, plus garden varieties such as 'Alba Grandiflora', 'Blue Ice', 'Fujiyama' (white), 'Harlequin' (lilac, variegated), 'Prince of Orange', 'White Admiral'.

Polygonatum × hybridum Solomon's Seal

Flowering time: Late spring and early summer.

Foliage: Rich green, shiny and pointed, on long arching stems.

Height: Up to 90cm (3ft)

Spread: 45cm (18in) or more

Positioning: 30–45cm (12–18in) apart in fertile soil in shade; in beds and borders, near water and under deciduous trees.

Planting time: Autumn or spring.

Propagation: Sow seeds in a cold frame in spring; divide creeping rhizomes in autumn or spring.

Care: Best left alone to multiply quietly. Mulch drier soils in spring with garden compost, and check regularly in summer for sawfly caterpillars.

Recommended: Basic species, plus double form 'Flore Pleno' and less vigorous variegated 'Striatum'; P. odoratum and its many garden forms, and taller P. biflorum (syn. P. commutatum, P. giganteum) are also good in shade.

POLYGONATUM × HYBRIDUM

Sometimes known as P. multiflorum (although the true plant of this name is a different species), this lovely graceful plant is a native of woodlands and thrives in any kind of shade, soon spreading into large patches where happy.

Primula vulgaris (Common) Primrose

PRIMULA VULGARIS

New leaves start rising from the dormant crowns in late winter, a promise that the welcome flowers will follow soon after. This is not a plant for formal gardens, but deserves generous naturalizing wherever it can self-seed and multiply as if in the wild.

Flowering time: Early to mid-spring.
Foliage: Bright green, long, oval and leathery with deep veins.
Height: 15cm (6in)
Spread: 30cm (12in)
Positioning: 23–30cm (9–12in) apart in drifts, best in moist heavy soil but tolerates other kinds; in a cool semi-shaded site in orchards, hedge bottoms and wild gardens, and on grassy banks.
Planting time: Autumn or late winter.
Propagation: Sow seeds in a cold frame in autumn; divide plants in spring.
Care: Mulch with garden compost in spring and water in dry seasons.
Recommended: The true species is best; also double white 'Alba Plena', subspecies *sibthorpii* (lilac pink) and coloured garden forms. Various kinds of polyanthus (*P.* Pruhonicensis Hybrids) can be bedded out for spring display in semi-shade.

Prunus laurocerasus Cherry Laurel

Flowering time: Mid- to late spring.
Foliage: Long and narrow, glossy dark green.
Height: 90cm–1.2m (3–4ft)
Spread: 1.8m (6ft)
Positioning: Almost any kind of soil except chalk; as specimen shrubs, or planted 60–90cm (2–3ft) apart as ground cover or a low hedge.
Planting time: Autumn or spring.
Propagation: Grow semi-ripe cuttings in a cold frame in late summer.
Care: Shorten growth by one-third in spring a year after planting to encourage bushy growth; older bushes may be cut back hard in spring. Trim hedges in late summer.
Recommended: Other suitable cherry laurel varieties include 'Rotundiflora' (rounded leaves) and 'Zabeliana' (low spreading growth). For chalky soils the Portugal Laurel *P. hispanica* is a safer choice, especially the white-edged form 'Variegata', both making neat shrubs with white flowers in early summer.

PRUNUS LAUROCERASUS 'OTTO LUYKEN'

This very tolerant and adaptable variety grows almost anywhere, its tough leaves providing reliable ground cover. The attractive flowers are particularly conspicuous in full shade. Leaves and stems are poisonous if crushed.

Pulmonaria longifolia Lungwort

PULMONARIA LONGIFOLIA

There are several Lungworts that cross-fertilize readily. This is one of the most elegant varieties, but all kinds will grow contentedly in part or full shade and most are more or less evergreen, with attractively spotted leaves.

Flowering time: Mid- to late spring.
Foliage: Long, slender and pointed, dark green with white spots.
Height: 30cm (12in)
Spread: 45cm (18in)
Positioning: 30cm (12in) apart, in well-drained soils in full or semi-shade; as ground cover and under spring-flowering shrubs.
Planting time: Autumn or spring.
Propagation: Divide plants in autumn or early spring. Sow seeds (species only) in a cold frame in mid-spring and transplant outdoors when large enough to move. If plants set seed this is worth sowing, but seedlings usually will be variable hybrids, so grow in a nursery bed and select the best for planting in the garden.
Care: Mulch with garden compost in spring on lighter soils, and water in dry seasons.
Recommended: Basic species, or 'Bertram Anderson' (violet-blue flowers); garden forms of *P. angustifolia, officinalis, rubra* and *saccharata* are all good for shade.

Pyracantha coccinea Firethorn

Flowering time: Early summer.

Foliage: Rich green, neat, oval and shiny, on strong thorny branches.

Height: 3m (10ft), higher against walls

Spread: 3m (10ft)

Positioning: Most well-drained soils, in light or semi-shade; as specimen shrubs, free-standing or against walls, and planted 60cm (2ft) apart as hedges.

Planting time: Autumn or spring.

Propagation: Grow semi-ripe cuttings in a cold frame in late summer.

Care: Clip to shape in late winter; against walls trim back to the berries after flowering and tie in new shoots.

Recommended: 'Red Column' (upright) and 'Red Cushion' (compact) are good reds; other garden hybrids worth trying include 'Golden Charmer' and 'Soleil d'Or' (both yellow), and 'Orange Glow' and 'Teton' (both orange).

PYRACANTHA COCCINEA 'LALANDIA'

With their red, orange or yellow berries, Firethorns are excellent for brightening up the garden in autumn. They are extremely tough, useful as impenetrable hedging but also ideal for training in decorative shapes such as mopheads and espaliers.

65

Rhododendron Rhododendron

RHODODENDRON 'ELIZABETH'

Most rhododendrons are prone to sun-scorch and frost damage, and so appreciate the shelter of dappled shade. Almost all need acid conditions and are best grown in specially made raised beds or in containers where soils contain lime.

Flowering time: Mid- and late spring.

Foliage: Dark green, glossy, rectangular and pointed.

Height: 90cm–1.5m (3–5ft)

Spread: 1.2m (4ft)

Positioning: Well-drained lime-free soil with plenty of humus, in light shade sheltered from cold winds and frost; as specimens in acid or raised beds and containers, and in woodland settings.

Planting time: Autumn or spring.

Propagation: Layer in autumn or spring.

Care: Mulch every spring with a thick layer of decayed leaves or chipped bark. Deadhead to encourage new shoots. Water plants with yellowing leaves with sequestered iron and rainwater.

Recommended: Many varieties prefer light shade, including 'Blue Diamond', 'Curlew' (pale yellow), 'May Day' (orange-scarlet), 'Pink Drift', 'Scarlet Wonder', and the numerous *R. yakushimanum* hybrids.

Ribes sanguineum Flowering Currant

RIBES SANGUINEUM 'BROCKLEBANKII'

Flowering time:	Mid- to late spring.
Foliage:	Pale golden green, maple-shaped with incised veins.
Height:	90cm–1.2m (3–4ft)
Spread:	90cm (3ft)
Positioning:	Most soils that are not very dry or waterlogged, in light shade; in mixed borders or under deciduous trees.
Planting time:	Autumn or spring.
Propagation:	Grow hardwood cuttings outdoors in autumn or winter.
Care:	Mulch annually in spring with garden compost. Prune after flowering, removing one-third of all old stems to encourage new growth from the base.
Recommended:	'Pulborough Scarlet Variegated' is good in shade and 'Tydeman's White' might be worth trying. Also try R. laurifolium, (evergreen with pale green flowers), and yellow-flowered R. odoratum (Buffalo Currant). Red and white currants fruit well trained on shady walls.

Close relatives of the fruiting blackcurrant, flowering currants share the same habit and fragrance, and are equally tolerant of light shade. Whereas green-leaved forms may not flower quite so well in shade, golden forms prefer protection from the sun.

Rosa Climbing Rose

ROSA 'MAIGOLD'

A shady wall may be a blessing for climbing and rambler roses, which can suffer from heat and lack of water. Older roses often succeed here, many of them flowering once in early summer but often repeating later in the year.

Flowering time: Early to mid-summer; some varieties intermittently all season or with an autumn repeat.

Foliage: Fresh or dark green, often shiny, divided into several small leaflets, in most cases on thorny stems.

Height: Up to 9m (30ft)

Spread: Up to 6m (20ft)

Positioning: Fertile well-drained soils with plenty of humus; against fences and walls or where they can scramble into trees.

Planting time: Late autumn.

Propagation: Hardwood cuttings outdoors in early autumn; grafting in spring on to selected rootstocks.

Care: Mulch in autumn with well-rotted manure. Train in strong stems as they grow. Habit and needs vary with variety, so consult a good rose book regarding pruning.

Recommended: Many varieties including 'Bobbie James' (cream rambler), 'Danse du Feu' (fiery red), 'Lawrence Johnston' (semi-double yellow).

Saxifraga × urbium London Pride

Flowering time: Late spring and early summer.

Foliage: Spoon-shaped leaves in rosettes, mid-green with red undersides, serrated and leathery.

Height: 30cm (12in)

Spread: 15–23cm (6–9in)

Positioning: 15cm (6in) apart, in well-drained soil and light or semi-shade; as ground cover and edging, in rock gardens, crevices and containers.

Planting time: Autumn or spring.

Propagation: Divide rosettes in autumn or spring.

Care: Undemanding. Divide when clumps become overcrowded.

Recommended: One of London Pride's parents, *S. umbrosa*, is equally good for shade, as are *S. x geum*, *S. fortunei* and the many mossy saxifrages – these are forms of *S. geranoides*, *S. hypnoides* and *S. trifurcata*. All develop into mossy cushions of tight green rosettes and bear large red, pink or white flowers on thin wiry stalks.

SAXIFRAGA × URBIUM

A familiar edging plant in cottage gardens, where established clumps often merge to produce a rich and pretty strip of foliage beside paths. Sometimes offered under the name *S. umbrosa*, although this is strictly a different species.

Scilla nutans (English) Bluebell

SCILLA NUTANS

Patches of rich blue (occasionally white or pink) sparkling in the shade of woodland trees are part of the spring scene, and suggest where to grow Bluebells in the garden. Position them where other plants hide the sprawling foliage as it dies down. (syn. *Hyacinthoides non-scriptus*, *Endymion non-scriptus*.)

Flowering time: Mid- and late spring.
Foliage: Rich green, long, narrow and lax in clumps.
Height: 30cm (12in)
Spread: 30cm (12in)
Positioning: 10cm (4in) apart and 10cm (4in) deep, in groups and drifts, on most soils in light or semi-shade; in borders, wild gardens and under deciduous trees.
Planting time: Late summer and early autumn.
Propagation: Divide clumps in late summer; sow ripe seeds in boxes in a cold frame.
Care: Undemanding. Do not clear foliage until it has completely withered. Deadhead to prevent excessive seeding. Plants are best left undisturbed after planting to find their ideal depth (the bulbs are self-adjusting with contractile roots) and to form dense clumps which will only need division after several years.
Recommended: Basic species only; others prefer full sun, except *S. hispanicus* (Spanish Bell).

Flowering time: Mid-summer to early autumn.

Foliage: Bright green, oval or heart-shaped, downy with toothed edges.

Height: 12m (40ft)

Spread: 3m (10ft) or more

Positioning: Any soil in full or semi-shade, against high walls or trees.

Planting time: Autumn or spring.

Propagation: Sow seeds under glass in spring; grow semi-ripe cuttings in a cold frame in late summer.

Care: Although self-clinging, new plants may benefit from tying in at first. No pruning needed except to limit growth.

Recommended: Basic species only; the similar yellow-flowered S. hydrangeoides and its pink form 'Roseum' also enjoy shaded sites. Closely related climbers include Hydrangea petiolaris, with lace-cap flowers in summer, Decumaria barbara (confusingly known as Climbing Hydrangea) and the evergreen Pileostegia viburnoides; all are white-flowered.

SCHIZOPHRAGMA INTEGRIFOLIUM

Similar to the climbing hydrangea, using aerial roots to support itself, but it is more vigorous and bears larger heads of creamy blooms. For the best flowers, try to arrange a plant with its roots in the shade and its top in the sun.

Skimmia japonica Skimmia

SKIMMIA JAPONICA 'RUBELLA'

A male skimmia clone popular for its red buds that last all winter, finally opening as white blooms in spring. Other skimmias are male, female (long-lasting berries in autumn) or bisexual, bearing both male and female flowers.

Flowering time: Early and mid-spring.
Foliage: Dark green with red edges, elliptical, pointed and aromatic.
Height: 90cm (3ft)
Spread: 90cm (3ft)
Positioning: Most soils (preferably moist and not chalky), in semi-shade or sun; as specimen bushes in borders and containers, and planted 45cm (18in) apart as a low semi-formal hedge.
Planting time: Autumn or spring.
Propagation: Grow semi-ripe cuttings under glass in summer; grow hardwood cuttings in a cold frame in autumn.
Care: Mulch with decayed leaves or chipped bark in spring. Do not deadhead female varieties. Overgrown plants may be cut back almost to ground level in spring.
Recommended: Many other forms, including 'Bowles' Dwarf' (compact, male or female), 'Fragrans' (male), *S. reevesiana* 'Robert Fortune' (bisexual).

Tiarella cordifolia Foam Flower

Flowering time:	Mid-spring to early summer.
Foliage:	Light green, large and heart-shaped, copper-tinted in autumn.
Height:	15–30cm (6–12in)
Spread:	30cm (12in) or more
Positioning:	Any humus-rich soil that does not dry out, in shade or semi-shade; in borders, shrubberies and woodland, and in cool rock-garden sites
Planting time:	Autumn or spring.
Propagation:	Division in autumn or spring.
Care:	Cut down coloured leaves in spring to make way for new growth, and mulch with garden compost or leaf mould.
Recommended:	Basic species; also T. polyphylla 'Moorgrün' (green all year) and T. wherryi (russet red in autumn). Two similar plants are Tellima grandiflora (False Alum Root, Fringe Cups) with rounded heart-shaped leaves that turn red in autumn, and Mitella caulescens (Bishop's Cap) with bright green leaves and pale yellow flowers in late spring.

TIARELLA CORDIFOLIA

Excellent spreading and decorative ground cover that is almost evergreen – the leaves of most varieties assume autumn tints, from reds and browns to rich purple, and remain until the fresh green foliage overtakes them in spring.

Trachystemon orientalis Trachystemon

TRACHYSTEMON ORIENTALIS

This is a member of the borage family, with similar starry blue flowers that appear on hairy branching stems well before the large handsome leaves, which start to appear just in time to hide the fading blooms.

Flowering time: Early to mid-spring.

Foliage: Large, hairy and heart-shaped.

Height: 30–45cm (12–18in)

Spread: 60cm (24in)

Positioning: Almost any soil, in semi-shade or full sun; as ground cover for large bare areas or under deciduous trees

Planting time: Autumn or spring.

Propagation: Divide plants in autumn or late spring.

Care: Undemanding. May prove too vigorous for confined areas and will then need cutting back to size with a spade.

Recommended: Basic species only. This was once known as *Borago orientalis*. The true herb borage is a sun-loving annual for dry sites, but another species, *B. pygmaea* (syn. *B. laxiflora*) is a perennial with similar uses. It has graceful nodding sprays of sky-blue star-shaped flowers which last most of the season. Although slightly tender, it is a natural woodlander that self-seeds freely in rough infertile soils.

Trillium sessile Wood Lily, Toadshade

Flowering time: Early spring.
Foliage: Dark green, mottled and marbled with grey, long, oval and without stalks.
Height: 45cm (18in)
Spread: 30cm (12in)
Positioning: 23cm (9in) apart and 8cm (3in) deep, in moist leafy soil that is slightly acid; in cool dappled shade under shrubs and trees.
Planting time: Late summer and early autumn.
Propagation: Sow seeds in a cold frame in autumn (slow germination); divide plants after flowering, replant before rhizomes dry out.
Care: Mulch in winter with garden compost or leaf mould, especially on drier soils. Plants multiply slowly, so do not divide too often.
Recommended: Basic species only; try also T. chloropetalum (pink, red and white forms), white T. grandiflorum (Wake Robin) and its double form 'Flore Pleno', and yellow T. luteum.

TRILLIUM SESSILE

These are fragrant flowers and lovely in vases, although there are rarely enough of them for cutting. Highly prized, they are sadly slow to establish and multiply. It is worth making the effort to try to imitate their native woodland habitat.

Tulipa greigii
Dwarf Tulip, Species Tulip

TULIPA GREIGII 'RED RIDING HOOD'

Greigii and Fosteriana tulips are excellent for bedding out in light shade for bright spring colour. They are best treated as seasonal plants; lift and replanting each year so that they ripen well in summer.

Flowering time:	Mid- to late spring.
Foliage:	Broad and pointed, bright or dark green, often with reddish-brown stripes, the leaf bases enclose the stems.
Height:	20–45cm (8–18in)
Spread:	10–15cm (4–6in)
Positioning:	15cm (6in) deep and 10–15cm (4–6in) apart in groups, in any fertile well-drained soil in light shade or full sun; in borders, rock gardens and containers, and as formal edging.
Planting time:	Late autumn.
Propagation:	Sow seeds (species only) in a cold frame in autumn; detach offsets (small bulbs) at lifting time and replant in boxes or a nursery bed.
Care:	Although the bulbs may survive from year to year in good soil, they need a hot dry spell in summer; bulbs in shade are best lifted for drying off when the leaves have died down.
Recommended:	Numerous good hybrids, among them *T. fosteriana* 'Cantata', 'Golden Emperor', 'Juan', 'Madame Lefeber', 'Princeps'.

Viburnum tinus Laurustinus

Flowering time: Late autumn to early spring.

Foliage: Glossy dark green, oval and leathery.

Height: 1.8–3m (6–10ft)

Spread: 1.8–3m (6–10ft)

Positioning: Deep fertile soil, not too dry or wet, in light shade or full sun with shelter from cold winds; as specimens in borders and large containers, and also planted 90cm (3ft) apart as a hedge.

Planting time: Early autumn or spring.

Propagation: Grow semi-ripe cuttings under glass in summer; grow hardwood cuttings in a cold frame in autumn; layer in spring.

Care: Mulch with garden compost in spring on drier soils. Cut back vigorous branches and generally trim to shape in mid-spring.

Recommended: 'Eve Price' (pink flowers in late winter), 'French White' and 'Lucidum' (large white heads in spring) are also happy in light shade; variegated forms need full sun.

VIBURNUM TINUS 'GWENLLIAN'

This is the best evergreen viburnum for shady positions, where it is trouble-free and easy to grow. The pretty flowers, deep pink in bud, appear during the darkest months and last for 20 weeks or more, followed by metallic blue-black berries.

VINCA MINOR 'VARIEGATA'

Sturdy plants for difficult sites that are very dry or wet, or heavily shaded. Choose varieties with care as some may be very rampant on good soils, spreading by as much as 60cm (2ft) each year once they are well established. (syn. *V. m. variegata*.)

Flowering time: Early to late spring, and again in autumn.

Foliage: Glossy dark green, oval or lance-shaped, sometimes with silver or golden markings.

Height: 30cm (12in)

Spread: Up to 1.8m (6ft)

Positioning: 45cm (18in) apart, on any soil in shade or full sun; as ground cover under trees and shrubs, and also in shaded containers.

Planting time: Autumn or spring.

Propagation: Grow semi-ripe cuttings under glass in summer; divide plants in autumn or spring; layer at any time.

Care: Do not plant too deeply as stems may rot. Shear all stems back to ground level after main flowering or in late winter.

Recommended: Basic species (blue flowers intermittently all year), 'Azurea Flore Pleno' (double blue), 'Bowles' Variety' (large blue), 'Gertrude Jekyll' (white), 'Multiplex' (double purple); any of the many variegated forms; *V. major* and its varieties are taller and more vigorous.

Flowering time: Mid to late spring.
Foliage: More or less evergreen, small, rounded or heart-shaped in clumps, dark green with a purple tint.
Height: 8–10cm (3–4in)
Spread: 30cm (12in) or more
Positioning: Almost any fertile soil, in light or semi-shade; under trees and shrubs, in wild-flower gardens or grass, and beside water.
Planting time: Spring.
Propagation: Sow ripe seeds in a cold frame in late summer; divide plants in spring.
Care: This can be very invasive on moister soils and may need chopping back during summer. Sweet violets need rich soil and annual division or mulching with garden compost.
Recommended: Other attractive species include *V. cornuta* (Horned Violet) and its varieties 'Alba' and 'Lilacina'; *V. elatior* (pale blue in summer), *V. sororia*, especially 'Freckles' (white with violet flecks).

VIOLA LABRADORICA PURPUREA GROUP

Just one of the many violas, including sweet violets (*V. odorata*), that are semi-woodland plants rejoicing in cool shade. Charming and easy-going, they often self-seed freely or spread (sometimes invasively) into dense leafy mats.

Waldsteinia ternata Golden Strawberry

WALDSTEINIA TERNATA

An attractive woodland plant with a refreshing appearance, spreading gently to form dense ground cover, but rarely invasive except in rich soils. The foliage is more or less evergreen, and retains its decorative value in almost any position.

Flowering time: Mid- to late spring.

Foliage: Bright green, leathery and divided into 3 lobes, like an evergreen strawberry.

Height: 20cm (8in)

Spread: 60cm (2ft) or more

Positioning: 30–45cm (12–18in) apart in moist leafy soil (but drier soils are tolerated), in full or semi-shade; as dense ground cover under trees and shrubs.

Planting time: Autumn or spring.

Propagation: Divide plants in autumn or spring; runners may be removed any time, although they are best rooted while still attached in the same way as strawberries, either direct into the soil or pegged into small pots.

Care: Undemanding. In small areas the creeping runners may need chopping back if they eventually become invasive.

Recommended: Basic species only; *W. geoides* (Golden Strawberry) is similar but does not spread by stolons and may be planted more closely.